W9-BDO-770

MIDNIGHT GARDEN
COLORING BOOK

Flower & Animal Designs on a Dramatic Black Background

LINDSEY BOYLAN

DOVER PUBLICATIONS, INC.
MINEOLA, NEW YORK

Copyright

Copyright © 2015 by Dover Publications, Inc.
All rights reserved.

Bibliographical Note

Midnight Garden Coloring Book, first published by Dover Publications, Inc., in 2015,
contains all of the plates from the following Dover books by Lindsey Boylan:
Midnight Garden Coloring Book (2015) and *Midnight Forest Coloring Book* (2015).

This 2015 edition printed for Barnes & Noble, Inc., by Dover Publications, Inc.

International Standard Book Number

ISBN-13: 978-0-486-80553-5
ISBN-10: 0-486-80553-0

Manufactured in the United States by RR Donnelley